THE
WOMAN
AT THE
TOMB

THE WOMAN AT THE TOMB

ABORTION AND REDEMPTION

JESSICA LOCKHART

DAVID LOVELL PUBLISHING
MELBOURNE AUSTRALIA

Published in 2017 by

David Lovell Publishing
PO Box 44 Kew East
Victoria 3102 Australia
tel/fax +61 3 9859 0000
publisher@davidlovellpublishing.com

Cover image: Rowan & Irene LeCompte, 'Mary Magdalene in the garden
with Jesus', mosaic mural in the Resurrection Chapel in the National
Cathedral, Washington, DC. Photo courtesy National Cathedral
Washington, used with permission.

Design by David Lovell Publishing
Typeset in 12.5/19 Bernhard Modern
This edition printed through Amazon Create Space

National Library of Australia card number
and ISBN 978 1 86355 164 9
Full Cataloguing-in-Publication details available from
the National Library of Australia

THIS BOOK IS DEDICATED
TO ALL WOMEN
WHO ARE SUFFERING
FROM ABORTION.

To protect the privacy of
my family and friends
the names of people
and some places
in this book
have been changed.

Acknowledgements

I am extremely grateful to Catherine Garrett, for her faithful listening, generous encouragement and detailed notes and advice on the writing of my story. I've learnt a great deal from you, Catherine. Thank you!

I would also like to thank my publisher, David Lovell, for giving me the opportunity to share my experience more widely through the creation of a beautifully designed book.

To my husband, my children and the people of this book, who have each, in their own way, helped me to turn round from the tomb of self and find life in the garden of faith – you have my eternal and joy-filled thanks.

O vis aeternitatis

Power of Eternity,
you who ordered all things in your heart,
through your Word all things are created
just as you willed,
and your very Word
calls forth flesh
in the shape
which was drawn from Adam.
Power of Eternity.
Power of Eternity.

Hildegard von Bingen
Canticles of Ecstasy

If we could know the future would we ever move towards it? Surely visions of suffering which is inevitable would prevent us from reaching for the joys to come. And so in not moving towards tomorrow would we be pushing back against the forward motion that is creation? It is this pushing back against creation that is, I think – in the language of my Christian faith – a sin. Ultimately, in my life, this sin is driven by the agony of not knowing. Anxiety, depression and manic episodes are all an expression of this. And yet is it possible to engage in the disastrous and tragic machinations of sin and then turn back into the forward motion that is creation?

In the Gospel of John, Mary Magdalene looks into the

tomb of Jesus and is shown by two angels that he is not in there. She 'turns round' to find a man standing in front of her. To begin with she assumes that he is the gardener. But when he calls her by her name 'Mary' she recognizes that the 'gardener' is actually the risen Christ. The tomb is empty of Life because Life is in the garden. And yet there are angels in that tomb.

In 2011 I had an abortion. I was married. I was a mother of two. I was Catholic. And I was in one of the most desperate and stressful times of my life.

When the doctor placed my first child, Lucinda, in my arms, umbilical cord still attached, blood and amniotic fluid still covering her, I looked into my baby's eyes and felt that I could see all the way back to the beginning of the universe – that moment when creation exploded and all worlds became possible. I never knew love, not in all its living force, until that moment with my first born child in my arms. Six weeks later, Lucy, my husband Simon and I moved to Dubai.

In the beginning motherhood was blissful. And while Dubai certainly proved to be a challenging place to live I was so wrapped up in my joy that the frustrations of expat life were easily smoothed over by the new life I had found as a mother. I quickly made strong connections with several other expat mums and, away from the crush of Sydney life, I flourished. For the first time in my life I felt I had reached a place of safety and that the years of pain, fear, loneliness and sorrow were gone forever. Within the year I was pregnant again and for the first few weeks of my pregnancy life continued in the gentle sunlight of settled motherhood.

It took several months after its take-off to reach us, but when it did the global financial crisis hit Dubai like a wrecking ball. The papers and online news sites were filled with story after story of collapsed construction projects. Simon was an architect at that time. He assured me, and perhaps he really believed it, that his project was safe and that meant his job was safe.

But, sure enough, one day he came home from the office and told me his project had been shelved and he was being made redundant. My equilibrium vanished. It wasn't because we were saying goodbye to 'The Sandpit', as expats call it. Actually I was thrilled at the thought of moving to London, the suggestion for Simon's next placement. It was that the personal financial chaos we thought we'd beaten was about to come careering back into our lives and the uncertainty that brought triggered what was to be a long descent into an all-too-familiar pit of psychological hell.

Some time after that day Simon and I were having a dreadful row. I became so angry that I screamed at him, kicked one of the baby gates clean out of the wall, and threw a cup of coffee on the ground so that coffee and crockery flew across the room. It woke Lucy who had been having her nap. I went into the nursery to settle her and the sight that met my eyes mortified me.

There was my baby standing up in her cot in her sleeping bag, holding on to the slats, dummy in mouth, shaking. I knew that the sounds of my rage had yanked my child out of her peaceful sleep and here she was crying in fright. I also knew that this rage was not new to me and that it would most likely occur again. I picked up my daughter and, cuddling and cooing to her, walked back into the living room to tell my husband that I needed to see a psychiatrist. I needed help with the rage, fear, pain, sorrow and unrelenting self-loathing that had hunted me, as wolves track their prey, all my life. I would not let any child of mine grow up in fear of the one person who was meant to be a place of absolute safety.

I went to my GP. She referred me to a psychiatrist who, after listening to me for several sessions, delivered a diagnosis that irrevocably shifted the axis of my world – bipolar II disorder and borderline personality disorder. According to her I'd had them for most of my life. Here was an explanation that would set me free. I was not, as I had always believed, worthless, despicable, hateful or unlovable. I was sick. Desperately, wreckingly sick. From that revelation to the understanding I have today, the way has been perilous. But what has been revealed to me is that, even for those who for most of their life have been unable to pick up their mat and walk, healing *is* possible.

The usual course of action after such a diagnosis is to go straight on to medication but since I was pregnant that was not an option for me. The alternative plan was really quite stark: get me through the pregnancy alive, deliver my new baby, and *then* get me on to medication. In the meantime my psychiatrist would see me at least once a week to help me navigate the manic-depressive storm our current uncertainties had unleashed inside me.

During that time, Simon and I had decided that Lucy and I would go back to Australia while Simon organized the transition from Dubai to London. For nine weeks I lived in my family-in-law's holiday house on the Mornington Peninsula. I don't know why we thought this would be the place for me. While there, I was tormented by searing loneliness that only compounded the dreadful uncertainty I was dealing with. Where was I going to have this baby? I looked into Queen Charlotte's Hospital in London. London fell through. A move to Muscat was considered. I didn't bother exploring options there because I was adamant that I would not give birth in Muscat. Thankfully Muscat fell through. Then a return to Sydney became a very real possibility so I booked myself into the Mater. Sydney fell through and I cancelled the booking. Then Melbourne as well and so I cancelled my booking at the Mercy Hospital.

I was five months pregnant when Simon managed to convince the Dubai office to cancel the redundancy and keep him on staff. I flew back to Dubai and booked myself into the American Hospital. Two months later, a second redundancy was proposed and again the London office beckoned. Our visas were settled but the client still hadn't signed the contract. I was heavily pregnant and facing the gruelling possibility of finding and setting up a home in a new country in the middle of winter. I started having visions of myself going into labour in the street in a blizzard with a toddler in tow. The longer the client delayed the more we realized that the London scenario was not really feasible. So, again, miraculously, Simon convinced his Dubai office to take him back.

In February 2010, after a traumatic episode with my obstetrician, Matilda was born. By then I had become so depressed that my psychiatrist had spoken to me about placing a suicide watch nurse in our home during Simon's office hours.

February passed. March too. April, May and June. The anti-depressants and mood stabilizer my psychiatrist and I had settled on started to have some effect. I remember picking up my now five-month-old baby one day, walking to the nursery to change her nappy and suddenly realizing that this little person was mine. She was my baby. I had helped make her and had held her in my body for nine months. She made us into our family of four. She was our second daughter, Lucy's little sister, my very own Tilda. The love that had, in those first few months, been present but hidden now flooded my heart and mind.

In July 2011 we decided that I would again return to

Australia to escape the Middle-Eastern summer. But this time the return would be permanent. My mother's twin sister, Clara, had died earlier that year from breast cancer and my mother had made the decision to sell the beautiful country property called Mountview that she and Clara had set up twenty years before and to move elsewhere. Not wanting to see the place which had played such a pivotal role in my early adulthood become lost to our family, Simon and I resolved to buy it. But first we would need to complete and sell the house we'd been planning for years on Sydney's north shore.

Forest Ave was going to be our dream home. Simon designed a beautiful house nestled into a high face of sandstone. It was the sort of house I had always dreamed of having. When finished it looked like something out of a lifestyle magazine and I must admit that for the brief time I lived in it I sometimes believed that it could have made an effective consolation prize.

The plan was that the girls and I would return to Australia and stay at Mountview with Mother until Forest Ave was finished and then the three of us would move up to Sydney and I would oversee the finishing touches and sale of the house, leaving us free to buy Mountview. Simon would stay in Dubai until his current project wound up. It would involve a period of living apart but in all truth I think we both secretly believed that would not be such a terrible thing. We had been falling apart for some months now.

About twelve months earlier Simon had started to lose weight and he was also becoming extremely tired. We both thought it was because of the stress of his uncertain work future. But by the middle of 2010 Simon had lost so much weight I was becoming convinced there were other factors at play. To begin with he wouldn't see a doctor. He was adamant that the problem was 'just stress' and on one occasion he even named me as the main cause for his stress. I suppose we were a large part of each other's stress, really.

While there had been some progress for me under medication, I still had not fully emerged from the bipolar episode I'd suffered during and after my pregnancy. Simon's ailing health was bringing me to believe that the future was uncertain in the worst way. I had to face alone the possibility that my husband, who had just turned fifty, wouldn't live to see fifty-one. He was so thin by then that I could see his rib cage poking through his back when he was in the shower and his thighs were the same width as his knees.

On a Christmas visit back to Australia that year two friends on separate occasions pulled me aside and asked me if Simon was okay, citing his terribly frail appearance as the cause for their concern. It was during that Christmas visit, when we again found ourselves on the Mornington Peninsula, that Simon came to me and said he could feel the staple in his knee from an old injury scraping against his bone and that he thought there might be something wrong with his weight and his health in general. He agreed that he needed to see a doctor and so we resolved that as soon as we were back in Dubai, which was only going to be a few days from then, he would book in with our GP.

The initial diagnosis was hormonal deficiency. He was placed on hormone replacement therapy and for the first few weeks we saw some improvement in his condition. He had more energy and started to gain weight. I can't say how thrilled we both were. It had been so simple a problem and now it was fixed. Hurrah! My husband was going to be okay. I wasn't a widow-in-waiting. Our little girls were not going to grow up fatherless.

But then the recovery plateaued. He was exhausted again and I saw the weight slipping off him. He went back to the doctor. It wasn't hormonal deficiency. That was only a symptom. 'Of what?' Stress was Simon's answer. 'And would you please just back off my health now, Jess? I don't want to hear about it any more. I'm just stressed and your badgering is making me worse.' So I backed off. I stopped urging him to seek help. And I watched in silence, which became anger, which became resentment and then contempt as the man I had married shrank, and declined, and continued to slip away from me.

On the evening before we flew out, our girls and I for good and Simon for a two week break, he told me that he had spent most of the last few days in hospital having tests done. Now the results were in. I held my breath, gathered myself in and prepared to hear my worst fears come true. I nearly cried with relief when my husband told me he had been diagnosed with diabetes. I had been expecting cancer. It was serious, yes. His doctors had told him that if he had let things slide for another month he would have fallen into a diabetic coma and then most likely died. His blood sugar level was five times higher than the normal limit. His body had stopped making insulin and his pancreas was pretty much ruined. But they could bring him back from that. And if he changed his lifestyle, mostly diet, he would not only survive but he could thrive.

The months of anger dropped away and I felt a flood of forgiveness. Finally my husband had gone to seek help. The disregard his stubbornness expressed for our security as a family and his denial of the reality of his ailing health had all been overcome. The reason? For two months before seeking help a second time he had begun to lose his eyesight and was starting to lose sensation in his feet. He was able to hide those symptoms from me because in my distress at his condition I had learned to look away.

Of course it occurred to me that I should cancel my exit from Dubai and oversee his return to health. But the dreaded Middle-Eastern summer was looming and that made apartment living with two feisty toddlers increasingly and unsustainably suffocating. It was time for me and the girls to leave Dubai and repatriate ourselves among the refreshing green and gently rolling hills of the Victorian countryside.

There are two moments which best describe the joys and the hardships of our first few months of living apart. One July morning I was dressing the girls in front of the fire at Mountview. Outside, a thick mist covered the garden and obscured the views beyond. Observing this Lucy said to me, 'Oh, Mummy, it looks really dusty today. We won't be able to go outside will we?' My heart swelled with joy as I hugged her and said, 'No Darling, it's not dust, it's mist, and we can go outside for as long as we like.' And with that I rugged us all up in jackets and boots, took my babies outside and cried with joy as I watched the girls jump and splash in the many muddy puddles Mountview had to offer that day.

But there was no joy in my tears the day that Simon left for the airport after his first visit back to us. Lucy, knowing that he was leaving, clung to him and begged him to take her with him. How could he explain that he couldn't? When he drove away she chased the car as fast as her three-year-old legs would carry her, screaming in tears, until he turned the bend in the drive and was out of sight. Again I collected her in my arms but this time sank to the ground and wept with her.

It had indeed been a wonderful visit. In the six weeks of our leaving Dubai and Simon's first visit to us he had regained some of the weight he had lost and he was looking and feeling quite well. He was now taking four insulin injections a day and his blood sugar readings were coming in at half what they had been at diagnosis. He had given up the cans of coke, cordial and bags of sweets that had been his energy boosters throughout his period of decline, and his happiness at seeing the girls and me with space around us and clean air to breathe was confirmation that this had been the right move.

I loved being at Mountview. Watching my children run with the wind in their hair and their cheeks bright with cold, clean air and listening to rain fall on the tin roof while curled up with a book in front of a crackling fire helped me leave behind the empty opulence and grating boredom of life in Dubai. Watching dawn blaze across the vast sky-filled view that makes Mountview a place of such beauty released me from the cruel gaze of a desert sun lurking behind a sulphur sky. And to go to Mass again, which was a practice I had given up during our time away because of the region's difficult and strange logistics, was a homecoming for my soul.

But it would be simplistic to think that all was well with us again. I was still traumatized by the uncertainty of our financial situation. We were already over budget and horribly behind schedule in the first few months of the Sydney build and I had developed a rattling distrust of my husband's ability to provide stability and protect us from adversity. I had also not recovered from the trauma of his decline and the sense of powerlessness his enforced silencing of me had created. No matter how hard I tried to fight them, depression, mania and anxiety still had me in their grip. We had also had to make the heart-wrenching decision to tell Mother that due to the problems and delays of the Sydney build we would not be able to buy Mountview.

When Mountview went on the market I think I felt that all options for a settled and happy existence had been exhausted. Then I discovered I was pregnant again. I had to abruptly stop taking medication because of the harmful effects it would have on the baby. Simon's lack of employment options had him trapped in Dubai and he was unable to come home to support me. I was struggling with single motherhood. My daughters' beauty had become obscured by the storms in my brain.

I felt alone in a dark wood on a dark night and I knew that this time the wolves had well and truly picked up my scent. Again I began to think of suicide.

The first phone call I made after the home pregnancy test proved positive was to a close friend of mine, Brian, who is a Jesuit priest. I think his was the first voice I wanted to hear because I had been told in no uncertain terms by my psychiatrist in Dubai that pregnancy while medicated was out of the question, and if it did occur her medical advice would be to abort. She cited studies of the effects my mood stabilizer would have on a foetus. She told me that the drug was severely teratogenic, which means it crosses the placenta and can cause major birth defects.

My psychiatrist in Australia had said pretty much the same thing but put me in contact with a man who specializes in the effects of drugs on unborn children. He came back with the conflicting news that at the dose I was taking any major birth defects would be highly unlikely. He even suggested that, rather than not take the drug at all, for the sake of my sanity I should go back on it. This was supported by the obstetrician I was seeing. She said my age – thirty-eight – posed more of a risk to the baby's health than the drugs I needed to keep me stable. Then one day when I was yet again crying uncontrollably in her clinic she said, 'Jess, is any baby appropriate for you right now?' And that was the crux of the matter. Healthy or not, I really, really felt that I could not cope on my own with another child at that time in my life.

It is always hard to draw an accurate picture of psycho-logical chaos. My life at that time was certainly filled with challenges that would make this pregnancy and a new baby quite stressful but it would be feeble of me to claim that those challenges were more than garden variety. However, in the same way that any person of unremarkable physical attributes can sit for an artist who goes on to make a portrait of quite marked distortions, a disordered mind can present even the most humdrum of circumstances as if they were the very obstacles that kept Odysseus flung far from his native home. This was also true of me.

Around this time a very dear friend of mine, Angela, had a baby. Her text message expressed gratitude and delight to be bringing this new child into the community that she and her family belonged to. In my depressed state I received her news like a kick in the guts. *I* had no community. *My* baby would not be born into any community. I didn't even have my husband. My baby would be born only to isolation and despair.

Never has loneliness gripped its slimy black claw more tightly around my heart than in that moment. I would be on my own with a new born child, two toddlers, an absent husband, the financial labyrinth of Forest Ave and the indescribable hell of self-loathing that continued to hammer me from inside. I had come to hate being a mother. I felt that I was doing a terrible job with my girls and I was plagued by fears of passing on to them, through my own sense of hopelessness, the horrors of constant sorrow and destructive manias.

At times I was an exultant mother, extravagant in affection and praise, lavishing on my girls the time and attention I had always craved as a child. But I could also be hard. The raw anarchy and constant neediness of very young children acted as a trigger for extreme irritation and a powerful need to withdraw. The shame and loathing I would feel when I shrieked in frustration at them or pushed them away and the constant feeling I had of parenting from the prison of my disordered mind caused me to fear that I was failing my children in the worst way. I had no idea which doctor to believe regarding the risks or otherwise of medication to the baby. I felt I had lived my life into a corner and that this pregnancy was the blow that would bring me down for the count.

All of these, said Angela, were great reasons not to get pregnant. But, she said, now that I was pregnant, they were irrelevant. Today I can see that she spoke the truth. Up against the mysteries of creation, worldly sufferings *are*, if not irrelevant, then at least secondary. But at the time her words, said in order to wrench me from the hell I was venturing into, released an avalanche of the feelings of irrelevance I had grown up with. I felt my life was over, so abortion or not the child would die. Should I have the baby and *then* flip the car? But then Simon would be left with a newborn as well as toddlers to raise on his own. The pressure of the build, his awful career prospects, a new baby and single parenting would probably kill him. And then the girls would be orphans. Who would raise them? What would become of them? Catastrophe! Catastrophe!

I was in a tail spin. I had completely lost control of my mind and my life and the worst part was that fundamentally I felt abandoned. Simon couldn't come back from Dubai. I suppose there were reasons enough for that but all my brain could understand was that he wasn't coming home to support me. And I couldn't go back to Dubai. The trauma of Tilda's birth still haunted me.

Certainly, I was living with my mother at the time but she was unable to cope with me being unable to cope and I suppose in a maternal protective sense was anxious for me to abort the child and return to medication. The two people a woman traditionally relies upon for support during pregnancy seemed to be unable to provide the support I needed. I became desperate. Tilda was due to be baptized up in Sydney on the coming Sunday. Simon was flying in for the celebration. So, slamming my mind shut against the grim irony of my plan, I booked myself in to abort the child on the day before the baptism.

The clinic was in Sydney's CBD. Simon dropped me at the door and took the girls out to lunch. I climbed the stairs to the clinic and became confused when I reached the door. It was a clinic for daytime cosmetic procedures. There was nothing on the door to indicate that abortions took place inside. I went back down the stairs and checked the building number against the address I had written down. It checked out so I climbed the stairs again. I opened the door and asked the woman at reception if I was in the right place and she assured me that I was. I filled out the forms and, waiting to be called in for my obligatory 'counselling' session, sat in the reception area trying to calm my nerves.

During the session the counsellor, who could see that I was becoming very upset, tried to reassure me. I had told her that I was Catholic and she said, 'Don't worry about that. Lots of Catholic women have abortions. We have lots of sex workers in here who are Catholic and have abortions anyway. In fact I was raised a Catholic myself and if I told my mother where I work she'd disown me so don't worry about a thing.'

I was given a surgical gown to change into and when I closed the door on the change room I was starting to cry quite badly. I came out to walk into the operating theatre and passed two young nurses chatting loudly and laughing about their plans for that night. I sat on the edge of the operating table and the surgeon placed the tourniquet around my arm and tightened it. He picked up the needle which held the anaesthetic. For some reason I looked down to my left and there on a tray were the surgical instruments that would be used to destroy the foetus and suction it out of my womb. A primal cry made me sit up and say, 'NO! Not my baby.' The surgeon and nurses removed the tourniquet and ushered me out to the recovery room. I sat crying and trying to calm myself before I called Simon to come and collect me. I told him that I just couldn't do it and he said he was relieved. I didn't ask him why. The next day the four of us went to St Loyola's, the church where I had returned to faith, and had Tilda baptized by Brian.

During the sacrament of baptism the congregation, parents and god-parents of the child renew their baptismal vows. The priest asks, 'Do you reject Satan?' and we answer, 'I do.' That moment has always captured my imagination. When I say those words I can always perceive either faintly or profoundly where Satan currently manifests in my life. My heart and mind are always engaged in this part of the sacrament because I know that to reject Satan and all his empty promises is, in my personal experience, to reject a large part of what makes up the self.

So much of my faith life has been shaped by my struggles against the hell inside my brain. Deep in the caves where I have crawled for refuge from Satan's torments I have found jewels of wonder and awe. Over the many cliffs I have thrown myself to escape the chase of my demons I have felt myself being lifted as if the breath of the Spirit swept in to break my fall.

I have never known despair without grace. I have never been shoved into the solitary confinement of my mind-built prison without falling into the love of God's embrace. And so when Brian asked us all on that day if we reject Satan my response was, 'I don't how to.' Is this the true danger we place ourselves in when we allow ourselves to lose faith? If we don't pray are we leaving ourselves open to be preyed upon by all in our world that God is not? Pray or be prey. Perhaps that is the corner into which I had lived my life.

After the almost-abortion and the baptism, Simon flew back to Dubai and I returned to Mountview. I was traumatized by the absurdity of the experience at the abortion clinic in Sydney. I was alone. I was depressed. And I was torn. In one sense the pregnancy tied me to life. If I had this baby how could I kill myself? How could I leave Simon so burdened? The baby tethered me to life and what I wanted, what I ardently believed I wanted, was freedom from the hell I perceived my life to be. In my depression-stunted mind I believed suicide to be the only solution.

But of course in moments of clarity – and there were

some – if the baby tethered me to life then so did my daughters. After all, three kids or two, single parenting would be a terrible burden to place on Simon. And the other thing that stopped me was what kind of woman he might marry to raise the girls. Would she be Catholic? It was not likely that Simon would ever marry another Catholic. And then my girls would miss out on the beauty and richness that, rightly or wrongly, I have always believed is particular to Catholicism. I was raised by parents whose Christian humanism provided for an extraordinarily rich, even sumptuous, experience of Catholicism. What would my girls have? Secularism? Spiritual poverty?

But even in this state I still managed to find moments of light. I remember one such occasion when I packed a picnic lunch and took a rug down to the park in town with the girls. I played with them on the play equipment and lavished attention on them. Feeling tired, I left them to continue their adventures while I took some time out on the rug. It was a perfect spring day. The girls were playing happily with each other and with other children in the park. Dotted around the place were mothers with babies also watching their older children play. It suddenly occurred to me that perhaps things would work out all right. Maybe I could do this on my own. It wasn't long though before I slipped off that ledge and plummeted into the pit where my ultimate decision was made.

I called Simon in Dubai. Crying, I told him that I had decided, finally, to abort my baby. The decision brought some relief. It was as if my hand was caught in a threshing machine with the rest of me about to be dragged through. The only way out was to hack off the limb that was caught. That limb wasn't the baby. It was my conscience. In order to kill the baby in my belly I had to first shut down that part of me which is a part of every human, which connects us unseverably to the great gift of our humanity – conscience. And there is no secular argument, regardless of its intended compassion, that can dispute what I knew in my heart to be true. Abortion is a perversion in the most fundamental sense because it is an act that deliberately causes death in a place that has been specifically designed to create life.

Simon flew home for that weekend. We left the girls at Mountview with Mother and drove into a Melbourne clinic where the abortion took place. As we got out of the car we met pro-life activists who trailed us up to the door, trying to put pamphlets into our hands. One woman said to me, 'Let me save your baby.' I felt like rounding on her. 'Will you move in with me? Help me with my toddlers? Walk with me? Be there for me? Be my partner?'

Perhaps not all women go through torment in the process of making this decision but very many do. It is an act which often takes place in desperation; desperation that springs up, claws and all, from whatever circumstances the woman finds herself to be in (often a lack of meaningful support): desperation that expresses itself in the urgent and immediate struggle for survival across every part of a woman's identity. I understand that the people who call for the preservation of life outside abortion clinics ultimately do so from compassionate motives. But when the hearts, minds and bodies of women are treated as inconsequential, even as a means to an end, compared to the life of the unborn, is the fullness of compassion really being met?

And yet … and yet …

We entered the clinic and immediately felt a sense of wrongness in being there. Simon expressed this. 'This is not right', he said. 'It's not us, Jess.' I thought to myself, 'us?' There was no 'us' in this. He wasn't living with me.

He wasn't there to help me with the daily grind. And I knew that to do what was 'right' would bring me to bear a burden I believed would kill me. My mind was made up. I was sick of wrestling with myself. I did not have the emotional or psychological strength to have this baby on my own. And so I held my conscience down by its throat, shoved a rag into its mouth and went through with the abortion.

The next day I went to Eucharist. Never before had I so needed the Embrace, the welcome, the love of my Lord Jesus as I did that day. Despite what Catholic morality and the catechism have to say about that I still thank God daily that I did go to Communion. I think it was the thing that, in all its mystery and beauty, gave me the strength to see what I was about to see. It was the last Eucharistic nourishment I would receive for some six weeks.

To begin with I felt nothing but relief. It was over. And I felt that perhaps I could find a way back to life. I started back on medication. I promised to be a more patient and kind mummy to the girls. I looked at the chaotic and fragmented situation my life was in and thought that at least without the awfulness of pregnancy and a looming baby I would be able to cope with things a bit better. Simon flew back to Dubai and I continued with life at Mountview.

It was mid-November. Christmas was approaching. Soon we would be in Advent. The Annunciation. The Nativity. And inside me Our Lady's 'Yes, Lord', and my 'No, Lord' began to grind into each other. A swell of shame and in-adequacy was rising over this ground zero and racing to the shore to get me. I stopped receiving Eucharist. I had come to see that this abortion, this killing, was the work of all that is deadly inside me and it had become hideous in my eyes.

But I had to have something. I think there is a pilot light inside us all that can't be reached and so can't be put out. It is the life spark that sits and waits even in the darkness and so long as it burns there can be some small hope that the purpose for which we were made can still be served. Despite the mangled state of my soul I ached for the Embrace so I continued to go up to the priest during the sacrament but kept my arms folded across my chest because the gospels tell us time and again that Jesus reaches out to gather in and hold close the wretched and unwell. And I have never felt this more keenly than in those weeks leading up to that Christmas.

All this paints a picture of a woman dragging herself and her sack of woes through days of grinding awfulness. It wasn't like that all the time. After all, I had two little girls to care for and they had their own life which I was insistent my rankness would not infect. So we continued to go to the park and to family day care where they could enjoy their little friends. I took them for walks, read to them and played with them, and made sure they had good food and proper bed times and only a little television. We did lots of cutting and pasting leading up to Christmas. We made decorations and they painted pieces of cardboard with glitter paint which I cut into the shapes of a nativity scene. We still have it and use it some Christmases. I still looked forward to Christmas at Mountview as Simon would be there and some of my siblings and a favourite cousin were coming to stay with their kids.

But racing alongside my functioning life, like dolphins diving in and out of the waves at the bow of a ship, was this tormented view of myself. It had always been there. The abortion had just given it a shape. And while I would never say the abortion itself was a good thing, I do say, with gratitude and great wonder, that much good has come from having entered so irrevocably into its reality.

Christmas came. Simon flew out from Dubai for two weeks, and several days before New Year's Eve we had one of the worst fights we've ever had. It was about all the usual things – Forest Ave, crushing debt, our shocking instability. I lost control, flying at him claws and all and then, realizing that to stay anywhere near him would put me in terrible danger of doing real harm, I threw some clothes in a bag and fled. I stayed at a friend's house that night and the next day fetched up at a Cistercian Abbey in one of Victoria's beautiful rural districts.

The Abbey was quiet. No husband or children demanding more than I had to give. Just peace and other adults come to seek time away in prayer. I remember putting myself to bed that night in the room that had been assigned to me. I had just shared in the evening meal with the other guests where conversation had been very grown-up indeed. I hadn't had to tell one person to 'hurry up and eat, get off the floor, pick that up, don't chew with your mouth open, let mummy eat', etc. Exhausted, I got into my pyjamas and scrubbed my teeth. I turned down my sheets and picked up a book I'd found on one of the bookshelves. I climbed into bed and as I did all these things I had an overwhelming feeling of being mothered, utterly cared for, nurtured. As though I was being put to bed by Jesus' mum and she was going to sit with me until I fell asleep.

How glorious to wake to the singing of psalms. My room overlooked the chapel and the monks were engaged in the Office of Vigils. Being summer and still dark I supposed it to be at least before five am. I stayed in bed listening to their voices and again had the sensation of being in a place of absolute safety, of being watched over by a motherly presence.

Some time after the singing finished and when I was sure I was quite rested I rose, showered and dressed, and walked down to the chapel for the six am Office of Lauds. Eucharist is offered during this time but still I felt shut out and, in a new environment, very shy. I opted out of approaching the priest with my arms folded across my chest. Breakfast followed and then I spent time reading and thinking and just sitting in the chapel enjoying the peace and quiet. The Office of Terce takes place at eight am and since I was still in the chapel I stayed as the monks filed in and sang their prayers. I had come to the right place. Even though I was still in torment I knew already that the rhythm of the Abbey was exactly the clock I needed to reset my heart and mind to. Afterwards, as I walked back to the guest house, I came to a decision.

At one of the meals on the previous day I had met the Abbott. As one of the few ordained men at the Abbey, he was able to offer the sacraments. I resolved to ask him if he would hear my confession. He said he would and later that day when I was sitting in the front room of the guest house he came to fetch me to a different room where I poured out my confession – the abortion and all the brokenness of my marriage.

The story took quite some time to tell and I spared no detail. The Abbot listened very attentively and when I finished he offered me the sacrament of reconciliation. I accepted with the gratitude of one who might take a glass of water after a long journey through a desert. I asked him if I could also receive Eucharist. 'Yes, of course', he said. I cried tears of relief and the next day, on New Year's Eve of 2011, I received Eucharist with the community at the Office of Lauds.

During my first day at the Abbey I had met a woman called Rachel. She was a lay sister and a mother of grown-up children. She had a bright and sunny disposition and I warmed to her instantly. She had been the one who showed me to my room and pointed me towards the bookshelves. She had informed me of the ins and outs of the Abbey and had winked in conspiracy while one of the guests droned on and on over the evening meal about his many virtues. This man (unmarried and childless) had even offered me advice on being a parent, at which Rachel raised one eyebrow and beamed me the sort of smile that only an experienced mother can offer an exhausted mother of two intrepid toddlers.

That evening, Rachel introduced me to Brother Joshua. We were making our way back from Compline in the summer twilight when there he was, standing on the front porch of the guest house, enjoying the fresh air that had swept in after the day's blistering heat. I remember Brother Joshua's lilting voice as the conversation meandered and I found myself telling him about the overwhelming sensation of being nurtured I'd had on my first night at the Abbey. He looked me square in the eyes and said, 'That was Grace, Jess; you were experiencing Grace.'

The next morning, New Year's Day, it was time to say goodbye to the Abbey and to drive myself to the airport where I would board a plane for Sydney to hear Brian say his last Mass at St Loyola's. After nearly two decades of ministry, Brian was retiring from parish life to take a year-long sabbatical. This was bitter-sweet for many of us who were his current or former parishioners. Of course it is always good to know that a cherished friend is taking a much needed rest, but it was very hard to calm the sense of loss I felt that Brian would no longer be at the church where I had come back to faith. I had always experienced my friendship with Brian as a sort of father/daughter relationship and knew it to be unique in my life. He was also the one person I felt could intercede for me with God and I quickly developed a fear that he was intending to leave the church completely. He assured me he wasn't.

Brian had been a friend of my parents when I was just a little girl. Friendship between him and my father grew over the years. Then, in 2001, after I had returned to my faith after many years away, my father introduced me to him. There was an experience I needed to clear up before I felt I could fully participate in the Mass. Brian and I went up to a local cafe and he listened to me. It was one of the first times in my life I can remember feeling completely listened to. After I had finished speaking Brian asked me if I would like to receive the sacrament of reconciliation. We walked back down to the presbytery and there, in his office crowded with books, Brian brought me home to the church. I felt a great, dark cloak slip from my shoulders and I was free.

The next time I saw Brian was at Mass and I was struck not only by the effort that went into the music but also by the very personal way Brian offered the liturgy. I was also rather delighted by the eccentricity of a priest saying Mass in bare feet. Brian, above all things, is kind. And that kindness flows through his Masses to create the sort of intimacy I have always imagined being present in the upper room at the last supper. Shortly after meeting Brian I was quite mercilessly dumped by a man I'd had some hope in. I had called Brian in floods of tears and that very night he met me for dinner at a small sidewalk Thai place near his church. I told him that this man had broken with me because he thought I had too many problems. Brian said, 'Jess, you have mysteries, not problems', and again I was struck by the kindness in him.

I felt that Brian had opened a door for me and on the threshold was Jesus and Jesus, I began to realize, loved me and accepted me and wanted me and would walk with me and hold my hand and be there for me. Jesus would be kind to me. And my first experience of that kindness was Brian. I became a parishioner at St Loyola's. Since then Brian has confirmed me, married me to Simon, baptized both our children and walked with me to absolution for countless wrong turns.

So it was an essential pilgrimage for me to fly from the Abbey to Sydney and celebrate with Brian his last Mass at St Loyola's. Many people were reaching for their hankies by the end of it. I couldn't stay for the lunch that followed as I had to catch a flight home. Back at Mountview that night I received a text from Brian thanking me for flying up especially for the Mass. He described it as an 'extravagant and generous' gesture. But actually it was nothing more than what he'd given me as a friend especially in the lead up to and the aftermath of the abortion.

I mentioned earlier that Brian was the first person I called when I discovered I was pregnant. It was an instinctual reaching out to the one person I knew would be really true with me in this matter and not hit me with agendas or ideologies. What Brian did was try to help me listen to the good news of the pregnancy, to hear the Annunciation. But in my depression I rejected all he laid before me and listened, instead, to the hell inside my brain.

When I called Brian a week after having the abortion he said, 'Well, Jess, I know this has been a very tough and painful decision for you to make and I just want you to know that I am in your corner. I really mean that, Jess. I'm in your corner.' I don't think I'd ever heard those words or even that sentiment expressed to me before. Brian's gentleness in this moment was the same gentleness I had come to experience in Jesus and again I was filled with wonder and awe at Christ's love for me. I had done something that at a secular level made perfect sense but at a spiritual level was a very serious sin. I had hammered a big, bloody nail into the cross by my lack of trust in life and yet Life itself was in my corner.

One day early in the new year of 2012, I was attending weekday Mass in the town close to Mountview. At the end of the Mass the parish priest asked if some of us could stay behind to help pack up the nativity setting. A few of us did and everyone picked up a figure to take back to the storage cupboard. The only figure left when I got to the altar was Our Lady. I picked her up in my arms. The irony was not lost on me. Here was I, a woman who said 'No, Lord' carrying in my arms a statue of the woman whose 'Yes, Lord' gave us a new creation. It was one of those moments I often have when I feel immensely grateful to be Catholic and to be able to see in true light my path of fear and faith.

By the end of January 2012 I had moved up to Sydney to the new house. Because I had grown up in the next suburb I decided to return to the church my parents and I attended during my early adolescence. This decision was not blasé. At different times we had been members of two churches in the area, but St Dominic's on the upper North Shore was significant to me because it was the place where, at fourteen, I had decided to leave the faith. That decision was made on exactly the same instruction, 'pray', that saw me come back to the faith at the age of twenty-seven.

When I was fourteen I belonged to the youth group that met every Sunday night at St Dominic's in the newly-created diocese of Broken Bay. The leader of the youth group was a boy called Tom. Tom attended a local Catholic boys' school and we were both part of the wider community of Catholic kids in that area. I wasn't the only girl with an intense crush on Tom. He was tall and dark haired and as well as being dreadfully good looking he was extremely charismatic and terribly, terribly cool. His other attribute, as many of us girls knew but hated to admit, was that he was a bully and a ring-leader with a cruel streak.

On the last evening I ever attended this group I arrived at

the annexe to the church and there on the door I was greeted by my name written into the dust with the words 'is a slut' after it. I knew who had written them and when I confronted Tom he didn't deny it. On the contrary he laughed at the effect of his efforts. I stopped attending the youth group and my parents, concerned at the anguish Tom had caused me, booked me in for a chat with one of the clergy of the parish. When the priest patted me kindly on the knee and said, 'Don't worry, dear, just pray to God and he will fix everything up for you', I lost my faith in prayer.

A few days later I told my parents I had decided to stop attending Mass. I had always delighted in the Mass as a child. It captured not only my theatrical side but also my instinctual relationship with Spirit from a very young age. My parents knew this and they also knew that this experience had been a terrible violation for me. They accepted my decision without question.

Fast forward another twelve years and I found myself living and studying in Perth. Having recovered from an alcoholic breakdown the year before in Melbourne, I had completely stopped drinking. As irony would have it, however, the apartment I rented was opposite a bottle shop.

Usually this didn't bother me. I'd had such a rock bottom with drink that I wasn't going to be easily enticed to take it up again. But one evening I found myself craving a drink. I wasn't a member of AA and had no one to reach out to and no strategies in place to help me deal with the power of the thirst.

I remember pacing the floor of my apartment with purse in hand knowing that if I went across the road and picked up a drink I was unlikely to put it down until damage had been done in my present life. I said out loud, 'What am I supposed to do with this?' and a single word dropped into my head. 'Pray'. So I sank to my knees and I prayed and I prayed and I prayed and eventually the thirst was lifted. 'Just pray to God and he will fix everything up for you.' This was the moment that began my long and bumpy road back to faith.

By 2012, St Dominic's priest was Father Peter. Father Peter is a wonderfully scholarly person whose vast knowledge not only of the faith but of the world in general allows him to preach homilies that open up the beautiful meanings and great richness of the Word. His Masses are like carefully prepared love letters to God and he celebrates Mass with a perfect balance of delight and solemnity. Of all the things I miss about living in Sydney it is his Masses and Brian's that tug at me the most. I went to Mass daily because hearing the Word gave me just enough nourishment to get through my life a day at a time. But for me the Mass was also filled with triggers and snares. Even as I marvelled at the richness and glorious beauty of Catholicism I would stumble and tear my feet on its undergrowth.

As my faith became more intimate so did horror, shame and loathing for what I had done. All around me were proofs of my inadequacy. At that church there were many mothers with large families. On Sundays I would watch these women with their husbands and children and I would think about my total inability to manage just two little girls, my inability to bring my husband to Mass, my lifelong inability to be happy and my total and utter failure through having an abortion.

One of these mums, Emily, was a very beautiful woman with sparkling eyes. I had been to her home for dinner one night and met her husband and children. Her daughters were attending the same Catholic school I had been to. And while the evening had been a joyful gathering of their friends and family I felt myself a stain on their loveliness. Succumbing to a glacial loneliness I left early with my stomach tied up in knots.

I remember seeing Emily at the hardware store one afternoon. She was standing just outside with whatever it was she had bought and I stood at the checkout with my length of rope (I had been learning how to tie a noose via the internet). I listened to her delight at the result of her latest homemaking project. She was like sunlight. I wanted to say hello to her. I wanted *her* to say, 'Oh hi, Jess, what's the rope for?' I wanted to tell her it was for hanging myself. Instead I walked past her, got into my car with my rope in my hand and went home to continue my grim studies.

Another woman I met was Gloria. She introduced herself to me one morning after weekday Mass. She became a very good friend to me; one of those people whose presence in my life brings me to see that God is watching over me. She was very supportive and seemed to really understand the difficulties I was facing both externally and internally. It is always refreshing to meet and spend time with people who courageously live their faith.

As a mother of eight children ranging from teenage years to adulthood she often gave me very practical advice and support which would help me take a few more steps through each of my most difficult days. I remember on several occasions when I hadn't been able to make it to Mass on a Sunday she called to say she was coming over to pick up the girls and give me a few hours rest. Lucy and Tilda loved this, I think. They needed a break from me as much as I needed a break from them. It was Gloria, with her faith, friendship and strong instinct for the suffering of others, who saved my life.

But even while I burned and writhed in my faith I also felt more alive in it than I had ever felt before. Life in Sydney was, I think, becoming a fire of purification for me. The relief I felt at certain moments in the Mass was like a cool hand across my forehead. Reciting the Apostles Creed, where it says that Christ descended into hell, always gave me the powerful image of Christ standing behind me in hell on the edge of a great precipice with his arms around my middle, allowing me to peer over the edge, to see the full horror of my sins, without falling into the abyss. I felt that this was one of God's great mercies, to send Christ into hell with us so that we can see the truth of our sinfulness and then return to life with him, alive with truth but unharmed. I started going to Adoration on Friday nights. I would dress up as if going on a date. I would kneel in the gentle light of the church, breathe in the incense, allow my heart and mind to be carried into the Sorrowful Mysteries which are always contemplated with Friday's Rosary.

In a world where we're too often forced to arrange our faces and say I'm okay, you're okay, everything's okay, it is a relief to take part in the penitential rite and say the words 'through my fault, through my fault, through my most griev-ous fault.' When the priest says, 'We lift up our hearts', I can feel myself strain under the weight of my own heart, offering it to God. 'Here. Take it. I can't carry it any more.'

I remember being at Mass one day and hearing as if for the first time the priest saying, 'You are indeed holy, O Lord, the fount of all holiness. Send down your Spirit upon these gifts like the dewfall ...' it snapped me back to a morning when I had woken at Mountview and stood out the front of the house watching dawn spread through the valley while cattle lowed and birds called and dew sparkled on the grass at my feet. There had been a sense of first creation and of something holy waking up the land, miraculously making itself known to me. To me! All these were the kindly hands by which I could come to accept, not only the abortion, but all the many failings of my life. I was in hell, but Christ was right behind me.

It is difficult to explain how this awakening to beauty could be happening at the same time as the gnawing despair I felt about my life. The only way I can describe my dance with Death is that Death is a very compelling suitor. I felt the hopelessness of my life closing around me. My marriage was all but dead, I couldn't cope with my toddlers, we were grindingly in debt and I was lonelier than I had ever been. I suppose the thing to do was to reach out for help and I did on many occasions but always with the sense that nothing could really help except non-existence. And very often the only prayer I could muster was a broken and savage keening of the heart.

Forest Ave was a long way from finished and we were by now so gaspingly mortgaged that it seemed as if we would never be able to complete and sell it. Simon was travelling from Dubai every few weeks and most of that period of my life was a fog of stress and uncertainty. In February we celebrated Tilda's second birthday. Simon flew in from Dubai and we had some friends and family over for the afternoon. I had been looking forward to the day as I've always enjoyed celebrating the girls' birthdays.

When Simon arrived he was complaining of pain in his abdomen. He spent the entire Saturday afternoon of Tilda's party and the next day throwing up in our bathroom. His blood sugar was climbing and nothing he did could bring it down. On the Monday I took him to hospital, worried that he was showing signs of diabetic ketoacidosis. The doctor warned he needed to stay in bed for a few days at least. Instead he boarded a plane the next day and flew back to Dubai. When he arrived at his office he realized he had become very sick and took himself to hospital where he spent the next five days throwing up blood. Eventually the doctors diagnosed a kidney stone. It was seven millimetres thick. The doctors at the hospital left him to battle it out on his own before they performed surgery to break it into smaller, more passable stones. During this time I was torn between staying home to care for the girls and flying to Dubai to care for my husband. As always, I chose the girls. My father-in-law went in my stead and Simon began to make some recovery. We all breathed a sigh of relief. My husband had escaped death yet again.

For Easter 2012, I decided to make a retreat at a monastery south of Sydney. At Easter Saturday Mass, when it came time to say the Lord's Prayer, the priest asked the congregation to join hands. As we did, a series of memories flooded my mind. I remembered a woman whose husband had recently died saying the same prayer at Mass at St Loyola's with her adult children either side of her, holding her hands as if to hold her up, her grief slamming into me from across the church. I felt the gift of it.

I remembered my hand as a child reaching out to hold God's hand on my nightly chore of emptying the compost bucket, so that he would protect me from the monsters my older brothers had convinced me lived behind the compost heap. I thought of a photo Simon took when Lucy was born of the doctor's gloved hands passing her across my belly into my outstretched hands. I thought of the sweetness of Tilda's habit of having to suck on the middle fingers of her left hand to get to sleep. I saw hands depicted holding each other inside a red circle with a line through it on any door to a public space in Dubai and remembered the little ritual Simon and I had of deliberately joining our hands as soon as any flight we were on had left the UAE. I decided to drive home that night and not wait until morning. Simon had flown over from Dubai to take care of the girls and I wanted to see him.

When I arrived home, I soon realized my error. We were sitting up in bed, later, discussing various things about the house and it was then that he told me that he had decided to complete the last two bedrooms and bathroom himself. My heart sank. Though he said it would only take a couple of weekends I knew that it was more likely to take months. I was desperate to get the place finished and sold. I wanted our time there to come to an end so that we could move on and find some stability at last. We had words about it and Simon became angry with me. He turned out his light with a very terse and ironical 'Happy Easter' and with those two words undid in a second what I had spent the last three days timidly trying to grasp. Hope.

I suppose a well mind could have taken all this on but I wasn't well. In fact I was sicker than I had ever been. I was pinging from mania to depression to mania and back to depression sometimes within hours or even minutes and there were many days when I seemed to live the two states at the same time. All this despite being on an anti-depressant, a mood stabilizer, an anti-psychotic and a sedative. But since that Easter Saturday night there had been one improvement in my life. I now had a purpose and a goal of my own. I started to draft a final letter to family and friends. It included the usual things: who to speak, which readings and which hymns to be sung, where to be buried, etc.

There were also instructions to the girls. It was for them, after all, that I was planning to take my life. I had really come to believe that I needed to step aside and allow a better woman to take my place. I loved them both immeasurably. I felt they were old enough to be permanently psychologically harmed by me and that the only way to protect them from this was to take myself out of their lives altogether. In fact it was my ardent hope that their memory of me would be vague at worst and at best non-existent.

The stressors of my life became a blur as I began what I was planning to be my final months alive. Not even the gentle ministrations of a treasured family friend who was living with us at the time could pull me from my despair. I gave up trying to be anything. My poor girls were often presented with vegemite on toast in front of the TV for dinner. I remember giving them popcorn for dinner on a few occasions while I would curl up on the couch and stare at the children's programs that had become their night-time bed and bath routine. All I could rouse myself for was Mass. And I would sit in the pew and be at once tortured by all that the liturgy showed me I was not and awed by, but certainly not hopeful of, all that the liturgy said I could be.

Finally, the house reached completion. We put it on the market and I think for Simon this was a relief because it meant the end of a lot of hassle and heartache. For me it was a relief because it meant that I could choose for my suicide the date I had hoped for, my birthday. I reasoned that it would make the grieving process tidier. Instead of my birthday *and then* the anniversary of my death in the years to come, the whole ordeal could be efficiently grieved on one day. I have always liked tidiness.

But then something happened that jammed a splinter of hope into my heart and mind. As my birthday approached, I noticed that its date falls on the same date as the feast of Our Lady of Sorrows. I had already felt in the story of my life a strong connection to Saint Mary Magdalene and because of this, when I was twenty-eight, I had chosen her as my confirmation saint.

My confirmation took place in December 2002. Earlier that year, I found myself living alone in a terrace house in Sydney's eastern suburbs. The people I had been living with had moved on, and, because the flat I had rented in an inner suburb on Sydney's harbour was not yet available, I remained in the house for several weeks. Towards the end of this period, on the afternoon of Easter Saturday, I had been to the ballet with my aunt. Since I was planning to attend Easter Vigil Mass at St Mary's Cathedral that evening I had decided to while away the hours between by seeing a movie. But as I was walking to the cinema a terrible depression descended on me and I found myself sitting on a bench in Hyde Park debating whether or not I should instead go down to the cliffs near my home and step off.

Then I heard a voice. Someone said, 'Can I talk to you about Jesus?' The question shocked me out of my thoughts, and when I looked up a young man was standing in front of me. 'Yes', I said. He sat down beside me and asked what I was doing and why I was looking so sad. I told him that I couldn't decide whether to live or die. The young man said, 'It's not your decision to make. God will decide when it's time for you to die.' As he began to talk about the passionate love Jesus has for me I felt myself being lifted out of the pit. We spoke until day faded into dusk. When he said goodbye it was time to go to Mass.

I entered the Cathedral with a crowd of worshippers for the Liturgy of Light, my heart and mind ablaze with the resurrection of Christ.

Some days later I went to see Father Brian to tell him what had happened to me. He said, 'You were one of the women at the tomb.' Soon after that, as I was preparing for confirmation, I realized that Saint Mary Magdalene had been with me, not just on that night, but through all the nights of my life.

So, in 2012, when I saw that my birthday – and what I was planning to be my 'death-day' – would fall on the feast of Our Lady of Sorrows, again I felt a sense of being called to life by the Christian narrative which has set my imagination on fire since early childhood. I had a sudden strong instinct that somehow God knew me, knew what I needed, knew what I was about. All my life God had given me Mary Magdalene, first witness to the resurrection, and here, now, God was showing me Mary, Mother of God, the first disciple. I had a sense that God was trying to reach me through all this suffering; trying to say something intimate to me by giving me this feast day as my date of birth. So I survived my birthday.

Then, two weeks later, on a weekend when Simon had decided to stay in Melbourne, where he was now working, and I found myself alone one Saturday night, Death slithered up the stairs of my brain and slunk into my resolve. I walked into the bathroom, picked up the bottle of Wellbutrin (Zyban), which was being supplied by my psychiatrist in Dubai and which still held about two months' supply, and swallowed the lot in a couple of fistfuls. I also took a few sheets of the anti-psychotic I was on and as much Valium as I had left.

I'm not sure what happened from that point. I know that it was my friend Gloria and her husband who took me to hospital. When I came to, I was in intensive care and had been in an induced coma for three days. Brian came to sit with me one day. It was extremely reassuring to have him near me. While in the coma it had been discovered that I had pneumonia and that that had probably been the cause of the repeated chest infections I'd been having over the past two years. After spending a few more days in hospital I went home and spent another week in bed to recover from the pneumonia once and for all.

The day after the overdose Simon came to Sydney to look after the children. But I think the emotional strain of my breakdown affected him quite badly and it was decided that the children would stay with Annette, his younger sister, until we were well clear of the more dramatic elements of our situation. Simon boarded a flight to Melbourne with the girls and deposited them safely into Annette's generous care. It would mean leaving me on my own for a day while he flew to Melbourne and back and since I was still very much a danger to myself another friend of mine, Karen, was posted in the house for the day to keep me safe.

Once I was well enough to travel, Simon and I drove down to Melbourne where I spent a further two weeks recovery in a private psychiatric hospital.

So what does life after all this death look like?

Since I came out of hospital we have sold the house in Sydney, bought and let go of Mountview and celebrated my fortieth birthday. Simon has changed careers and our daughters are in the early years of their schooling. In the five and a half years since the abortion we have narrowly scraped clear of bankruptcy, held on for dear life to a marriage which often feels like a tin boat in an ocean storm, and battled head on, again and again and again, the torments of my bedevilled head.

In the season of Lent 2015, I did a series of the *Spiritual*

Exercises at an Ignatian spirituality centre close to where I live. The Exercises were called Inner Peace in Divine Love. I did them because for some months I had felt myself slipping away from the church. I had stopped going to Mass because it had become too painful for me. The gnawing shame and regret I felt about the abortion was at the forefront of my heart and mind. It was becoming a schism between me and my commitment to being Catholic. I hid this behind the ruse of wanting to spend Sunday mornings with my husband and having too much to do during the week to attend weekday Masses. But truth, especially painful truth, cannot be ignored. Like a persistent child it tugged at my sleeve until it was attended to.

And for me the truth is this: I have always been a Catholic. I cannot *not* be Catholic. Even as a lapsed Catholic in my late teens and most of my twenties I was still a Catholic of some description. I could no sooner cancel being a Catholic from my identity than I could rip out my lungs and continue to breathe. The foundations of who I am, how I see, hear and taste the world are laid in the nightly reading of the gospel at my childhood dinner table and the discussions that followed those readings were, in their understandings, distinctly

Catholic. Catholicism is my core. It is how God reaches me. It is how God has searched for me. It is how God expresses an awesome and sometimes terrifying love for me. So it was time to ask questions again and examine the path I was on. After all, what sort of Catholic has an abortion?

The first week of the Exercises centres on memories of being loved. The second week is for dwelling on the love of Father, Son and Holy Spirit. That week's contemplations take place in the upper room of the last supper. You are asked to place yourself in the room with Jesus and the disciples. It was in the contemplations of this setting where I felt my relationship with God begin to breathe again.

In the last two weeks of the Exercises, each day concludes with an offering. We are asked what, in all reason and justice, we ought to offer and give to God. In my contemplations I was never able to answer this. Then, one day towards the end of the program, I was leaving the church, which is where, because of the lack of distraction, I preferred to do these Exercises, and the answer was given to me out of the air. 'Trust.' In all reason and justice the gift I can give to God is trust. It is a word, having been given in prayer, that I am now beginning to understand and make a habit of practising.

81

One of my favourite stories in Homer's *Odyssey* is when Odysseus and his crew are nearing the island where the sirens live. It is their job to lure men onto the island with their irresistible song and then kill them. Odysseus places wax in the ears of his crew and has them tie him to the mast of the ship so that he cannot, on hearing the sirens' call, steer his crew to destruction.

My mast is trust. Not only in some retrospective or penitential way relating to the abortion, although it is wise to understand the abortion through the prism of a lack of trust in life. But more urgently today to trust that perhaps it is God's strange gift to us to bind up so inseparably our experiences of suffering and grace. If I trust God I will be safe from the siren's call.

In the third week of Inner Peace in Divine love we are asked to contemplate our own creation in our mother's womb. We are offered Psalm 139:13-15.

> It was you who formed my inward parts;
> you knit me together in my mother's womb.
> I praise you, for I am fearfully and wonderfully made.
> Wonderful are your works that I know very well.
> My frame was not hidden from you

when I was being made in secret,
  intricately woven in the depths of the earth.

I fell down during this session. I had ripped apart what God had knit together. My spiritual director instructed me to redo this contemplation but this time to turn my ears away from Satan's taunts of the sin and bend my listening towards God's words of love for me. I did. And this time I fell open. In my revision of Psalm 139 I imagined the hands of Life taking each cell, dreaming its purpose, gracing it with the will to live and placing it next to another and another and another until a human is formed and then given to the world to continue, now in community, the great Good that is God's Word.

Late in the afternoon of that day I was standing out the front of my house. Watching dusk drape gently a velvet cloak over the view across the valley, I had a flash memory of Lucy's ten-week scan in my womb. Simon and I had seen a creature busy with life, furiously pumping and kicking the little buds that would become her arms and legs. We delighted in the idea that this could indicate what sort of person she would become. And it did. Lucy is a frantic, busy child who needs to move almost constantly. I realized that from the moment of conception a human person is present. A foetus is no mere clump of cells. It is a human being knitted together in its mother's womb.

The memory of Lucy in the womb didn't throw me into pain and guilt and shame for what I had done. Rather the understanding the memory brought helped me to accept God's forgiveness. I was able to say, 'Yes, Lord, I see it now. I see the gift that is Life. I see that it is *your* creation and that I am part of it.' I realized in that moment that I am, as we all are, beloved of God. But I am also, again as we all are, coveted by hell.

In the weeks after completing the Exercises I felt calmer and clearer than I have ever felt. Four weeks of intensive daily contemplative prayer had brought me to understand at an experiential level the necessity of prayer to my mental health. No pill had ever brought me to such clarity as those four weeks did. And it was for this reason, as well as unmanageable side effects, that I decided to ditch antidepressants. For me, they are drugs that create a synthesis of peace by incarcerating my wolves behind a glass wall. But these wolves are merely restrained, not tamed, and they can smash through at the slightest crack. In May 2015 I removed that glass wall. Over a period of almost two months I tapered down to zero dose. No matter how careful the decline, zero dose, when you finally get to it, is horrible. Brain-shivers, nausea, aches and pains, fire on the skin and arctic water in your veins. This is the first week or so. After that it does get better. While the aftershocks of withdrawal lasted for around a month, by the end of the second week I was able to drive and manage all the daily tasks that come with being a mother. I felt awake. I started writing again and it seemed to be flowing. I felt relieved to be free of the dosage merry-go-round that many people experience on anti-depressants and my state of mind was better than I had expected it to be.

But one day, late in July of that year, as I was pruning the apple trees in our orchard, I became aware of a howling in my mind. I'd been hearing it for days but, because it had been muffled by the rushing thoughts of mania that, for me, always precede a depressive episode, I hadn't recognized it. Now the mania was finished and the howling became more distinct. My wolves were back. They would sniff out and track the scent of all that is my life's blood; my marriage, my faith, and my love for my daughters. With hackles raised and drool swinging from glistening jaws they can rip apart my brain with a monologue of self-hatred, rage, terror and despair. I still operate. I still get through the tasks of my day. And my state is not like this one hundred per cent of the time. I still have moments of peace and clarity and I still enjoy the company of friends. But when the attack begins again these become like the small mercies of a cruel interrogator.

This has always been my life but having the abortion blew apart the false structures I have too often used to shelter from it. In the moment when the wolves came back I realized that this time there was no escape. This time I had to face the horror in my head. Because this was my life: depression, madness, blinding fear, paralysis, worthlessness, degradation, shame and savage insecurity. This was my moment at the tomb when I stooped to look inside.

Suddenly I saw what the angels have for so long been trying to show me. The Tomb is empty of Life. And I knew that if I wanted life, and wanted it in abundance, I had to turn myself round and I had to start now.

That's not to say that switching pills for prayer has been straightforward. It hasn't. I still have days when Death reaches out its appalling hand to me. And certainly it is wise to engage in a holistic treatment plan when it comes to mental illness. So I still take a small dose of my mood stabilizer. I stay active, I eat properly, I engage socially and I get plenty of rest. But prayer has become the foundation of these measures. And it is through prayer that I have become certain there is something very specific God is trying to tell us through the image of a man with his arms nailed open on a cross; suffering must be accepted if it is to become transformative.

Had I accepted the suffering I experienced during my last pregnancy, would I have gone through with the abortion? If I had accepted the agonies of my life in Sydney, would I have tried to kill myself? I'll never know. All I can do is take those questions and apply them to the hardships I experience today. I am learning to say, 'Let it be done to me according to thy word', because here's what else I've learned – the Word is good.

Sometimes, in my imagination, I see the child. She is like a phantom limb cut away but still demanding my attention. And she grows stronger with time. Not fading away into the fog of past mistakes but occasionally pressing her face up against the membrane of my consciousness. I always imagine her to be a 'her' because being a mother of girls makes it hard for me to imagine the aborted child as a boy.

The first time this happened was about four years after the abortion, on a perfect spring day. Simon and I were working on the cubby that Simon had built for the girls. Lucy and Tilda were jumping on the trampoline that sits in the middle of a circle of silver birch. A soft breeze fluttered through new leaves and dappled sun sparkled the light on my children's faces. They were holding hands and singing a song of their own invention. And suddenly, in my mind's eye, the child appeared, laughing in the breeze, her hands joined with Lucy and Tilda in their bright game.

I allowed the phantom child to amble over to me. To make a mess with the paint I was using. I allowed her to follow me when I took myself off to the garden bench under the beech trees that overlooked our dam. I allowed her to sit with me, to admonish me with the possibility of her aliveness. For the first time since the abortion I allowed myself to grieve. Here was another gift of grace. Now, as the child grows up in my imagination so do grief, regret, shame and remorse mature into quiet acceptance that what I did, I did in despair.

There is a moment in the third *Lord of the Rings* film between Aragorn, a ranger and heir to the throne of Gondor, and Elrond who is the King of the Elves. Elrond says something in elvish and Aragorn, also speaking in elvish, answers him. The translation is, 'I give hope to men. I keep none for myself.' It is the moment of change in Aragorn's spirit when he rises to meet his destiny. He casts off the survivalism of his ranger identity for good and embraces the sacrificial reality of his kingship. It has always been a goose-bump moment for me.

The reason I relate it now is that in recent months the sense of despair I have often felt since becoming a mother has started to shimmer and shift into the understanding that perhaps hope is a gift which lives not so much in the having but in the giving. Everything I do as a mother, even the glaring mistakes I make, is driven by my desire that Lucy and Tilda may always live in hope. Through motherhood I have experienced galling failure in myself. But it is in placing this sense of failure into the careful hands of my Christian faith that I have come to understand and accept the extreme sacrifice that mothering requires. I'm not just talking about scaling back careers or sleepless nights. Rather, for me, it has been a painful cutting away of the way in which I used to hope for wholeness.

Very often I feel as if all the hopes I ever had for myself have been blasted from me by the Theia-like impact of the love I have for my children. It is hard to express this thought because it runs contrary to the traditional idea that motherhood somehow completes us. Yet it is in submitting myself to the drudgerous wastelands of motherhood and in picking over the composted scraps of this discarded self, that something very new and quite surprising has been discovered. Just like the giant impact of the planet Theia that hit Earth all those billions of years ago, a total destruction of the structure of who I thought I was and who I thought I could be is being wrought.

That is a very painful process but it is also a very fruitful one. After all, that impact gave us our moon and the moon gives us our tides and the tides have helped to shape a world of magnificent diversity. Perhaps the smashing disruption that is motherhood is all part of the process of my formation into something infinitely more life-giving than the person I was before impact.

But if human experience of time is just a pin-prick in eternity then perhaps the relatively short hours of our lives are being lived by the spirit over billions of years. We are all dust of the universe. And so it must be not only through joy that we glimpse eternity but through grinding pain as well. And I wonder if it is this intuited sense of eternity and all that it brings that causes some of us to shriek an agonized 'No' to life. And after that 'No' an anti-*Magnificat* must be sung, a sort of dirge for the soul must be wept out in a place of desolation. No songs of joy for those of us who cower and claw and cover our ears against the Annunciation, but a cruel and rocky desert. Some of us may wander there, breaking our jaws and clogging our guts with the stones of false nourishment. But others may choose to 'turn round' into the embrace of God and back into creation.

Mary was standing outside near the tomb, weeping. Then, as she wept, she stooped to look inside, and saw two angels in white sitting where the body of Jesus had been, one at the head, the other at the feet.

They said, 'Woman, why are you weeping?'

'They have taken my Lord away,' she replied, 'and I don't know where they have put him.' As she said this she turned round and saw Jesus standing there, though she did not realize that it was Jesus.

Jesus said to her, 'Woman, why are you weeping? Who are you looking for?'

Supposing him to be the gardener, she said, 'Sir, if you have taken him away, tell me where you have put him, and I will go and remove him.'

Jesus said, 'Mary!' She turned round then and said to him in Hebrew, *'Rabbouni!'* which means Master.

John 20:11-16

As someone who lives with bipolar II disorder and borderline personality disorder, I spend much of my life weeping into the Tomb. But it is always and only when I stoop to look inside and answer the question the angels are asking me that I am able to turn around and hear Life, not Death, calling me by my name. Now I am learning to listen, and to listen deeply, to Life; with all my heart, with all my soul, with all my strength and with all my mind.

'The first stories I ever heard were the gospels' says **Jessica Lockhart**. 'My father would read the daily gospel to his family before dinner as a way of saying grace … That big, blue Bible held a world beyond my own filled with miracles and grand events and spoke of this extraordinary man who could heal people with the touch of his hands.'

Jessica's early involvement with the Scriptures was to return later in her life to help her heal from her grief over an abortion and to make sense of a lifetime of untreated mental illness. Today she has come to find some stability and peace.

'I have battled with mental illness for most of my life, and it is only in the last five years that I have felt any sense of true hope. My children and my faith have been the main drivers of that.'

Jessica has written for theatre and film and is currently working on her first novel. Apart from reading and writing, her main interests are her children, her friendships, and her faith.

www.ingramcontent.com/pod-product-compliance
Lightning Source LLC
Chambersburg PA
CBHW071953100426
42736CB00043B/3090